The Keepsake Bible Story Coloring Book

Emily Hunter

With Illustrations by the Author

HARVEST HOUSE PUBLISHERS
Eugene, Oregon 97402

The direct Scripture quotations in this book are taken from the King James Version of the Bible. Certain illustrations in this book are adapted from *The Bible-Time Nursery Rhyme Book* by Emily Hunter (Harvest House, 1981).

THE KEEPSAKE BIBLE STORY COLORING BOOK
Copyright © 1993 by Emily Hunter
Published by Harvest House Publishers
Eugene, Oregon 97402

ISBN 156507-001-1

Printed in the United States of America.

94 95 96 97 98 99 00 01 — 10 9 8 7 6 5 4 3 2 1

*Other Books
by the Same Author*

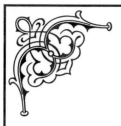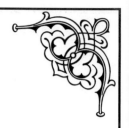

Contents

Part 1
Old Testament Bible Stories
with *Keepsake Pictures* to Color

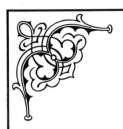
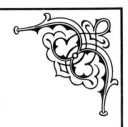

Part 2
New Testament Bible Stories
with *Keepsake Pictures* to Color

Part 3
My Very Own Keepsake Drawings
of the Wonderful World God Created

The drawings and coloring your children produce today
will become tomorrow's treasured keepsakes.

How to Use This Book

1. **Store this "keepsake" book apart from your children's other books.**
Make it a special occasion when you bring out this book. Explain to your children that a "keepsake" is something precious we keep for years and years. They will look forward to the times when they're allowed to color in their special book.

2. **Start your children coloring the pages at an early age.**
Don't wait until they've learned to "stay within the lines." To record your children's *progressive* development, preserve samples of their earliest attempts.

3. **Read the Bible story to your children before they color.**
In this way the Bible story will be reinforced in your children's minds as they color the characters. When they are finished coloring, review the previous Bible stories. The children will enjoy hearing them again as they view their previous colorings.

4. **Let your children color at regular intervals.**
This book can record your children's development over a number of years. Mark your desired weekly or monthly schedule on a calendar. Be flexible, however. Always let your children color on their birthdays. Then show them how they have improved since their last birthday.

5. **Encourage your child's creativity with original drawings.**
Beginning in Part 3, space is provided for your children to express themselves creatively by drawing their own pictures of God's wonderful world. When they are finished, ask them to tell you about it. Record their own words in the space provided. Reserve these pages until your children are able to draw recognizable objects.

6. **When the book is completed, store it among your treasured keepsakes.**
When grown, your children will delight in looking through this book. They will be glad you preserved their early accomplishments. You will be glad too. Though many children's creative expressions become wrinkled, dog-eared, and lost, you will have preserved an enduring record of your child's developing skills within this album.

———————

Part 1

OLD
TESTAMENT
BIBLE STORIES

with

Keepsake

Pictures

to
Color

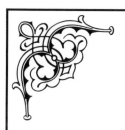
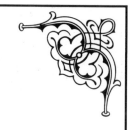

Adam and Eve
in the Garden of Eden
Genesis 2:7-25

Can you imagine how it would feel to be the only man on earth? In the beginning, that's what I was—the only man in the whole wide world!

I was the first person ever to see the sun or moon, the trees or flowers. I was the first person ever to see the many different kinds of animals God had made.

God told me to give names to the animals. All the animals were tame then. Even the lions and tigers were gentle. They came to me willingly, and I chose a special name for each one.

At first I was happy living among the animals in my garden home, but soon I began to feel lonely.

God said, "It is not good for man to be alone. I will make him a companion."

God put me into a deep sleep, took a rib from my side, and from the rib formed a woman. When I awoke, I was surprised to behold a lovely creature—like me, yet different.

How happy I was that God had given me this woman, Eve, to be my wife. Now I had someone to talk to, someone to eat with, someone to love. Together we watched the deer leaping through the woods. Together we listened to the birds singing in the treetops. Together we talked with God as we walked through the garden in the evenings.

Eve and I spoke no cross words to each other. We had no worries. We lived a perfect life in a perfect world, loving God and each other. Oh, how I wish it had never changed! But it did.

———————

Who created our beautiful world? Who created the animals? Who created Adam and Eve? Who created you? The Bible tells us that God created all things! Isn't God wonderful?

Colored By: _____

Date: _____

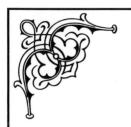
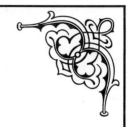

How the Snake Tempted Eve
to Disobey God
Genesis 3:1-24

"Good afternoon, Eve!" said the snake as he peered slyly from the forbidden tree. "Have you noticed this beautiful fruit? It looks delicious. Would you like a bite?"

"No!" replied Eve. "God says we can eat fruit from every other tree, but if we eat fruit from this tree, we shall die!"

The snake laughed scornfully. "God is wrong, Eve! You won't die. Instead you will become very wise." His voice was sweet and coaxing. "Go ahead, Eve. Take a bite!"

"I'd like to become wise," thought Eve. "And this fruit does look delicious. Yes, I'll take a bite!"

Just then Adam appeared. Eve said, "Adam, take a bite!" He did. At that moment both Adam and Eve knew that something horrible had happened to them.

"Oh, Adam!" cried Eve. "I've never felt like this before! Something has changed! I feel miserable and fearful!"

Adam said, "I do too!" They looked at each other strangely. Afar off they heard the voice of God calling to them. For the first time in their lives Adam and Eve were afraid to meet God. They ran away and hid.

When God found them, he said, "Because you have disobeyed me, you shall suffer misery and sorrow until the day you die."

What a sad day for Adam and Eve. They had to leave their perfect garden home and go out into a strange world. Angels with fiery swords stood by the gate to prevent them from ever returning to their beautiful Garden of Eden.

Why did Eve eat the forbidden fruit? Whose voice did she listen to—God's voice or the snake's? Whose voice did Adam listen to—God's voice or Eve's? Whose voice should we always listen to?

Colored By: _____

Date: _____

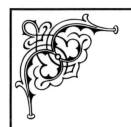
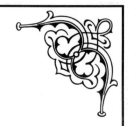

How God Saved Noah and the Animals
Genesis 6:1 to 9:17

All day long my hammer goes bang, bang, bang! What am I building? A big boat! My neighbors laugh at me. "Look at foolish Noah!" they say. "Does he think he can float a boat on dry land?" It's true, there's no water nearby, but God has told me a flood is coming. And I believe God.

Now I've driven my last nail. The ark is finally finished. I hear God's voice. He is telling me to bring my family into the ark, and to bring the animals, two by two.

That took some time, but we're all inside now! What do I hear? *Pitter-patter . . . pitter-patter!* It's raindrops! Now they're falling faster! It's pouring down!

Day after day it rains! Will the rain never stop? Every tree on the highest mountain is covered with water. But we are floating along in our big boat, safe and dry.

Finally the rain has stopped. The water is slowly going down. Yesterday I saw a mountaintop! Today I see a green tree! I can't wait to walk out on land once again.

At last the big day has come. We've been in this boat for more than a year, but now we're stepping out onto a world washed fresh and clean. It feels wonderful! The animals are happy too!

What's that arch in the sky? Look at the glowing colors—red, orange, yellow, green, and blue! Listen—God is speaking: "Whenever you see a rainbow," he says, "remember that I promise never again to send a flood to cover the earth." Thank you, God, for this promise. Thank you for saving our lives!

Why did the neighbors laugh at Noah? Did this stop Noah from doing what God had told him to do? If other children laugh at you for doing what is right and honest and good, what should you do?

Colored By: _____

Date: _____

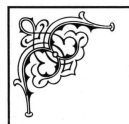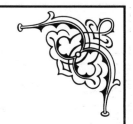

The Quarreling Shepherds
of Lot and Abraham
Genesis 13:1-18

Lot and his Uncle Abraham both owned large flocks of sheep. Every morning Lot's shepherds took their sheep out hunting for grass. Every morning Abraham's shepherds took their sheep out hunting for grass also. But they could never find enough grass for both flocks.

If Lot's shepherds found grass, they would not let Abraham's shepherds come near. "Go someplace else!" they shouted. "You can't feed your sheep here! There's hardly enough grass for Lot's sheep!"

And if Abraham's shepherds found grass, they would not let Lot's shepherds come near. "Get out of here!" they yelled. "This grass is for Abraham's sheep! You go find your own!"

Every day Abraham and Lot's shepherds fought. When Abraham heard of their quarrels, he was sad. He loved his nephew Lot and wanted no trouble between them. Finally Abraham said to Lot, "See all this land before us? Let's separate. If you take the land on the left, I'll take the land on the right. If you go to the right, then I'll go to the left. You may have first choice."

Lot looked out over the land. "I'll choose the best for myself!" he thought. "I'll take that green valley with the river flowing through it. My sheep will grow fat there, nibbling that nice green grass. The other land? It's all brown and rocky. My Uncle Abraham can have that!"

So Lot chose the best, and Uncle Abraham took what was left. But God promised unselfish Abraham a special blessing. "Look all around you," God said. "All the land you see I will give to you and your children and your grandchildren and all the children who follow them through the years forever and ever."

Why were the shepherds quarreling? Who was selfish—Abraham or Lot? Which one received a special blessing from God? Will God bless you for being kind and unselfish to others?

Colored By: _____

Date: _____

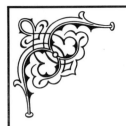
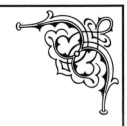

Jacob's Dream
of the Ladder to Heaven
Genesis 28:10-22

When you go to bed at night, would you like to lay your head on a rock instead of a pillow?

Of course not!

But one night I went to sleep on the ground, resting my head on a big stone.

I had been walking all day long in a lonely land. At sundown I looked for a place to sleep, but all I could find for a headrest was a big stone. I was weary from walking all day, so I fell asleep quickly—even with such a hard pillow.

That night I had a wonderful dream.

I dreamed that a ladder reached from the ground beside me and went up . . . up . . . through the sky into heaven. Angels were going up and down the ladder. Standing at the very top was God himself.

He spoke to me. "Jacob," he said, "I am the Lord God. I am the God of Abraham and your father Isaac. I am giving you this land. It shall belong to you and your children and their children and all the children that follow them forever and ever. I am with you, Jacob, and will watch over you wherever you go. I will never leave you."

When I awoke I said, "Surely the Lord is here in this very place."

I wanted always to remember God's wonderful promise and the place where I received it, so I took the stone I had rested my head on and stood it upright on the ground.

Then I made God a promise.

I said, "God, if you will always go with me and watch over me, you shall be my God."

———————————

God says, "I am with you and will keep you wherever you go" (from Genesis 28:15). Is God with you when you go to school? Is God with you when you go to your grandma's house? When you go to the doctor?

16

Colored By: _____

Date: _____

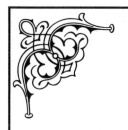
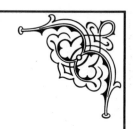

Joseph's Colored Coat
and His Jealous Brothers
Genesis 37:1-36

It's wrong for older brothers to treat a younger brother hatefully, but that's how my brothers treated me. Why? Because my father gave me a beautiful colored coat. This made my brothers jealous. They hated me.

One day my father said, "Joseph, take a message to your brothers who are tending sheep in the hills." I put on my colored coat and went on my way.

When my brothers saw me approaching, they said, "Here comes Joseph wearing that coat! Let's kill him and throw his body into a pit!"

"No, let's not kill him!" one brother argued. "Let's just throw him into a pit and let him die there." They agreed. When I arrived, my brothers seized me, tore off my coat, and threw me into a deep hole.

"Help! Pull me out!" I begged. They ignored my cries. Soon they saw merchants on camels passing by on their way to Egypt. One brother said, "Why let Joseph die? Let's sell him to these merchants." So they pulled me out of the pit and sold me to the merchants. The merchants carried me far away to Egypt.

My brothers quickly killed a goat. They took my coat and dipped it in the animal's blood. Then they carried my bloodstained coat back home to my father. "Could this be Joseph's coat?" they asked.

My father cried out, "Yes! It's Joseph's coat! He's been devoured by wild animals!" He was brokenhearted. "I shall go down to my grave mourning for my son!" he cried, sobbing bitter tears. My brothers stood there heartlessly watching my father grieving. They refused to tell him I was still alive.

_____

Why did Joseph's brothers mistreat him? Was it kind of them to let their grieving father think his beloved son Joseph was dead? The Bible says, "Be kind." Were they kind?

Colored By: _____

Date: _____

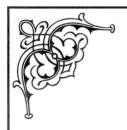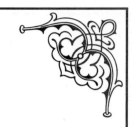

Joseph in Prison with the Baker and the Butler
Genesis 39:1 to 40:23

After my brothers sold me to the merchants, I was made a slave in Potiphar's house in Egypt.

One day Potiphar's wife said to her husband, "Joseph has acted wickedly toward me!" This was not true, but Potiphar believed his wife and threw me into prison.

While I was there, the king's baker and chief butler were also thrown into prison. One night they both dreamed strange dreams. "Tell me your dreams," I said. "God may give me their meaning."

The chief butler said, "I dreamed of a vine with three branches bringing forth grapes. I squeezed juice from the grapes into Pharaoh's cup and gave it to him to drink. What does this mean?"

"It means that you will return to the palace in three days," I replied. "Once again you will serve the king at his table. When you serve the king, please speak a word for me. Tell him I've done no wrong, yet here I am in prison."

Then the baker told me his dream. "I dreamed of three bread baskets on my head," he said. "The top basket held all kinds of bakery goods for the king, but birds came and ate them."

I sadly told the baker about his dream. "Your dream means you will be hanged in three days," I said, "and birds will come and eat your flesh."

Three days later the baker was hanged, and the butler was returned to the palace. I had hoped the butler would speak to the king about me, but he forgot. However, I knew that God had not forgotten me. I knew that someday God would deliver me out of this prison.

The picture shows Joseph telling the baker and butler about their dreams. Which man is the baker? The butler forgot about Joseph when he returned to the palace. Will God forget about Joseph?

Colored By: _____

Date: _____

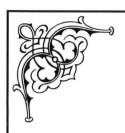
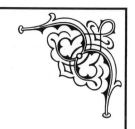

How Joseph Was Taken from Prison to the Palace
Genesis 41:1-44

Two years after the chief butler returned to the king's palace, God delivered me from prison in a marvelous way. This is how it happened: One night Pharaoh had a troubling dream. He called on his wise men to tell him the dream's meaning, but no one could tell him.

The chief butler spoke up. "I remember a young man named Joseph whom I met in prison," he said. "When the chief baker and I each had a strange dream, he told us their meaning. Everything came to pass just as he told us."

Pharaoh immediately sent servants to bring me to his palace. Pharaoh told me his dream. First he saw seven fat cows come up from the river and feed in the meadow. After that, seven thin cows came and ate up the seven fat cows. Then Pharaoh awoke. He fell asleep again and had a second dream. This time seven fat ears of corn came forth from one cornstalk. Then seven thin ears sprang up and devoured the seven fat ears of corn.

I told Pharaoh his dream meant there would be seven years of plenty followed by seven years of famine, when no grain would grow in his land. "Appoint a man who is very wise to see that grain is saved during the good years," I advised him. "Then your people will have grain to eat during the bad years."

Pharaoh said, "No one is wiser than you." So he appointed me to rule over all the land. Only Pharaoh was above me. He put his ring on my hand, dressed me in fine robes, and placed a gold chain around my neck. Who could imagine such a thing? In one day I was taken from the prison to the palace! In one day I became ruler over all Egypt with people bowing at my feet. What a wonder-working God I have!

Though Joseph had done no wrong, he was kept in prison for years. Did Joseph ever stop trusting God? How did God bring him from the prison to the palace?

Colored By: _____

Date: _____

23

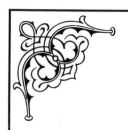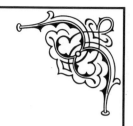

How Joseph's Brothers
Came to Egypt for Food
Genesis 41:53 to 45:15

After Pharaoh made me a ruler, I went throughout the land preparing storehouses for food. For the next seven years the land produced plenty. We packed the storehouses full of grain to feed us during the seven years of famine which lay ahead.

Finally the time came when no food would grow through all the earth. Hungry people from every land came to Egypt to buy food. When nothing would grow in Canaan, my father said to my brothers, "I hear there is corn in Egypt. Go there and buy some so we may live and not die."

So my brothers traveled to Egypt and bowed down before me. I recognized them, but they did not realize I was their brother, for I was no longer just a boy, but a grown man, dressed in royal robes.

When my brothers asked me to sell them food, I treated them harshly. I was testing them to see if their hearts had changed. "You are spies!" I said. "Into prison you must go!"

My frightened brothers whispered to one another. "All this has come upon us because of how we treated our brother Joseph. We should have been kind to him. God is now giving us what we deserve for the evil we did toward Joseph." I overheard their words and realized they were sorry for the way they had treated me. But I continued to test them.

When at last I was sure that their hearts were no longer cruel, I said, "I am your brother Joseph whom you sold into Egypt! Don't be afraid of me, for I forgive you!" Then we kissed one another and wept with joy.

Has your brother or sister ever treated you badly? Or perhaps a play-mate? If they tell you they are sorry, do you forgive them? Is this what Joseph did? Is this what God wants you to do?

Colored By: _____

Date: _____

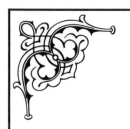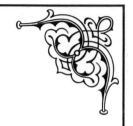

How the Israelites Became Slaves in Egypt
Genesis 46:1 to Exodus 1:22

When Pharaoh heard that Joseph's brothers had come to Egypt, he said to Joseph, "Tell your brothers to bring your father and all your family to Egypt. I will give them the best of my land—the good land of Goshen."

Joseph's brothers quickly returned home to tell their father the news. "My son is alive!" he cried with joy. "I'll see him before I die!"

So Joseph's father and brothers with their wives, children, and grandchildren came to Egypt bringing all their flocks, herds, and goods. Joseph rode out in his chariot to meet his father. What a happy reunion! They threw their arms around each other and wept for joy.

Joseph's family settled in the good land which Pharaoh gave them. They gradually grew into a great multitude of people. As the years went on, Joseph's father died and Joseph died also. Later a new king who had not known Joseph began to rule. When he saw his land filling up with the Hebrews, he became fearful. "These people are becoming great and mighty," he said. "Someday they could join with our enemies and fight against us. Let us deal harshly with them!"

So the new Pharaoh forced the Israelites into slavery. He made them work hard building cities and making bricks. If they grew weary and stopped to rest, cruel taskmasters beat them. When the king saw their families increasing in number, he ordered that every newborn son of the Hebrews be killed immediately.

As their lives became increasingly bitter, the Israelites cried out to God. God heard their cry. He heard their groanings. God had not forgotten them. He was preparing someone to become their deliverer.

Does God ever forget his children? Did God hear the cry of the Israelites when they were in trouble? Will he take care of those who love him? Will he take care of you?

Colored By: _____

Date: _____

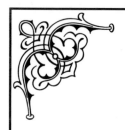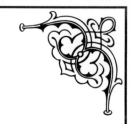

Little Baby Moses
Afloat in the Basket
Exodus 2:1-10

When you were a baby, did your mother ever set you afloat in a basket in a big river?

No, I am sure she did not! But that's exactly what my mother did to me. Why? To hide me from the wicked Pharaoh, who had ordered that all the Hebrew baby boys should be killed.

"Dear God," she prayed as she placed me in the big river, "please watch over my baby boy!" Then she walked sadly home.

Sister Miriam hid behind some tall reeds at the river's edge to watch over me. At first all was quiet. The water rocked my little basket-boat back and forth like a cradle. Soon I heard strange voices. The princess and her maids were coming down to the river to bathe.

I began to cry, "Waaa . . . waaa . . . WAAA!" Then I saw a face looking down at me. It wasn't my mother's face. It wasn't my sister Miriam's face. I was frightened!

"See what I've found!" cried the princess. "It's a baby boy! I want to keep him for my very own! I shall call him Moses!"

Sister Miriam ran quickly to the princess' side. "Won't you need a nurse for the baby?" she asked. "My mother can nurse him for you."

"Yes!" said the princess. "Take the baby to your mother. She can take care of him for me." So sister Miriam took me home to my own dear mother.

How good it felt to be cuddled in my mother's arms once again. My mother wiped a happy tear from her eyes and whispered, "Thank you, God, for taking care of my baby boy!"

Look at the picture. Who is hiding behind the tall grass? Why is she there? Was she a good helper? Do you have a younger brother or sister? If so, do you sometimes help your mother by watching over the younger ones in your family?

Colored By: _____

Date: _____

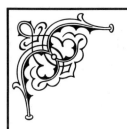
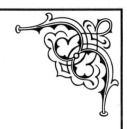

How God Spoke to Moses at the Burning Bush
Exodus 3:1 to 4:8

One day when I was tending my sheep alone in the desert, I saw a bush on fire. I waited to see it burn up, but it never did! It just kept flaming! As I stood in amazement beside the bush, a voice called, "Moses! Moses!"

I answered, "Here I am!"

The voice said, "You are standing on holy ground. I am the God of your fathers. I have seen the suffering of my people in Egypt. I want you to lead them to a good land where they will no longer be slaves."

"But Lord," I said, "that sounds like a hard job! I don't think I can do it! Besides, the people might not follow me. How would they know that you've sent me to them?"

God said, "What is that in your hand?"

"It's my shepherd's rod."

"Throw it on the ground!" he ordered. When my rod hit the ground, it became a snake. I ran from it!

God said, "Grab its tail!" I did. It became a rod again.

God said, "Put your hand inside your cloak, then draw it out." I did. White scales covered my hand.

God said, "Put it inside again and draw it out." I did. My hand was smooth and perfect.

God said, "My people will believe that I have sent you when you show them these miracles."

God's word was true. When I displayed these miracles to the people in Egypt, they believed that God had sent me and they rejoiced. "God has seen our misery," they said. "He wants to set us free!"

Do you remember how God saved Moses' life when he was a baby? Now he is grown and God wants to use him to lead his people out of Egypt. Does God have a special plan for your life too, even now while you are still young?

Colored By: _____

Date: _____

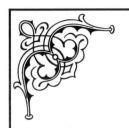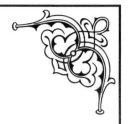

How God Forced Pharaoh to Let His People Go
Exodus 7:1 to 12:39

At last the time came for Moses to set his people free. He said to Pharaoh, "Our God demands that you let my people travel into the wilderness so they can worship him there." Pharaoh angrily refused.

God told Moses and Aaron to return to Pharaoh and show him signs and wonders so he would know their God had sent them. Aaron stretched out his rod, and rivers turned to blood. Frogs covered the land—frogs in the Egyptians' houses and frogs in their beds! Swarms of flies came forth. Cattle died. Sores came upon the people. Hailstones came down from the sky. Locusts devoured every plant. Darkness came over the earth for three days. But with each sign Pharaoh said, "No! I won't let your people go!" Finally he told Moses never to come see him again.

God said to Moses, "I will send one more disaster. Then Pharaoh will let your people go. Have your people kill a lamb and place its blood over the door of each house and on its side posts. Then have them roast the lamb and eat it, standing around their tables, packed and ready to leave. At midnight the oldest son in every Egyptian house will die. But I will pass over your houses when I see the blood on your doorposts. Your sons will be safe."

That night there was wailing and weeping as the oldest son in every Egyptian house died. Pharaoh's oldest son died, too. Pharaoh called Moses. "QUICK!" he cried. "Take your people and leave!"

That very night the Israelites marched out of Egypt—mothers, fathers, children—taking their belongings and flocks with them. With Moses as their leader, God was taking them to a new land which he had promised them—a good land where they would no longer be slaves.

How did God make Pharaoh change his mind and let the people go? What did Moses tell the Israelites to do in order to keep their oldest sons safe? Who was to lead them out of Egypt to the good land God had promised them?

Colored By: _____

Date: _____

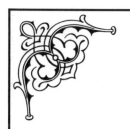
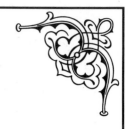

The Strange Cloud
That Moved in the Sky
Exodus 13:17-22

My brother and I were scurrying along beside our mother and father. We were hurrying out of Egypt, along with hundreds of other Israelite families. We were glad to be fleeing from the wicked Pharaoh who made our lives so hard. But everyone was wondering which way we should go.

As we hurried along, someone yelled, "Look up in the sky! Look at that strange cloud up there!"

Everyone's head turned up. "What does this mean?" they asked. "It's not like other clouds! It's shaped like a pillar!" As we were staring at the cloud, it began to move ahead of us.

"Come on! Let's follow it!" the people shouted. "God has sent the cloud to guide us!"

All day long we followed the white pillar of cloud. When the cloud moved, we moved. When the cloud stopped, we stopped. And when we needed to rest, the cloud hung over us like an umbrella to protect us from the heat of the sun.

"But how will we see the cloud when the sun goes down?" my mother asked. "How will we know which way to go?"

My father said, "Don't worry. God will take care of us." And he did. That evening when the sun went down, we looked up to find a brilliant red cloud glowing brightly over us in the dark! The fluffy white cloud we had followed during the day had changed into a glowing pillar of fire to guide us and give us light throughout the night.

"Isn't God good!" I told my brother. "God has given us a cloud to guide us both night and day!"

God cared for the Israelites during the bright sunny days and during the long dark nights, too. Does God care for you in the nighttime just as he does throughout the day?

Colored By: _____

Date: _____

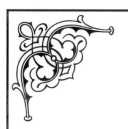
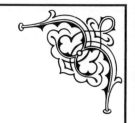

How God Made a Path Through the Red Sea
Exodus 14:9-31

"Mommy! Look at the water! It's heaped up high on each side of us! What keeps it up there? Why doesn't it come down? I'm glad it doesn't! If it did, we'd all drown! The water would pour over our heads and cover us all up! Ooh, this is exciting . . . but scary too!

"And daddy, look at the sand under our feet! It's dry! How can we walk on dry sand right in the middle of the sea?"

"It's a miracle, son! God is taking care of us. Remember how God led us out of Egypt away from that wicked Pharaoh? That was a miracle too."

"But Daddy, look behind us! See those men on horses and chariots? They're galloping fast toward the edge of the sea!"

"That's Pharaoh's army, son. They want to take us back to Egypt. They thought we would be trapped by the sea! But Moses stretched out his rod, a strong wind blew, and God separated the waters. Here we are passing through the sea on dry land. We're almost to the other side now!"

"But Daddy, when Pharaoh's army gets to the sea, won't they follow us on this path too?"

"Don't worry, son. God will take care of us. Here we are on the other side now. Praise God—we're all safely across!"

"Look back, Daddy! Pharaoh's army has entered our path! They're going to capture us! But look! The path is filling up with water. The waves are splashing over them!"

"Yes, son, our wonderful God has taken care of us again! He's saved us from our enemies! Thank you, God! Thank you!"

How did God save his people from Pharaoh's army? How did they cross the sea? Did they swim? Did they have a boat? Could God's enemies cross the sea too?

Colored By: _____

Date: _____

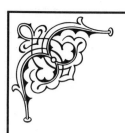
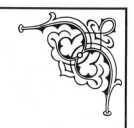

How God Rained Down
Manna from Heaven
Exodus 16:1-36

"Moses! Moses!" the angry people shouted. "We're hungry! There's no food here! Why did you bring us out here to starve to death? We wish we had never followed you into this wilderness. In Egypt we had plenty of food to eat!"

Moses knew it was God who had brought them out of Egypt, so he went alone to talk to God.

"God," he prayed, "what shall I do? How can I satisfy this hungry mob?"

God said, "Tell the people that in the evening they will have meat to eat, and in the morning I will rain down bread from heaven."

That very night a flock of quails flew over the camp, and everyone ate meat.

Early the next morning the people went out from their tents looking for bread. At first all they found on the ground was dew, but as the dew disappeared, they discovered small round clumps lying everywhere. They didn't know what it was, so they called it "manna."

Moses said, "This is the bread from heaven that God is giving you. Gather it, but don't take more than you need for today. If you keep it overnight, it will spoil. Every morning God will send you exactly what you need for the day."

The next morning the people went out and found more manna. Every morning manna appeared, and it tasted good, like honey wafers. How happy the people were! "Thank you, God!" they said. "Thank you for our daily bread!"

Have you eaten a slice of bread today? Did you have toast for breakfast? Or peanut-butter sandwiches for lunch? Did you say, "Thank you, God, for my daily bread"?

Colored By: _____

Date: _____

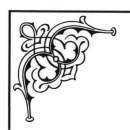
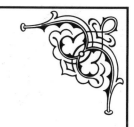

How God Gave Moses the Ten Commandments
Exodus 20:1-22; 24:12-18

One day as I was leading the people out of Egypt, we came upon a high mountain. As I stood gazing at it, God spoke to me.

"Moses," he said, "don't let your people touch this mountain. This is a special holy mountain where I will show my glory to the people."

We set up camp beside the mountain and waited.

One morning the sound of loud trumpet blasts burst from the top of the mountain. Everyone ran out of their tents. The mountain was shaking and quaking! Lightning was flashing and thunder was rolling! Smoke was billowing out in a huge cloud! We stood there amazed.

Then God spoke to us. His voice was like thunder.

"I am the Lord your God," he said. "I am the One who brought you out of Egypt where you were slaves."

He proceeded to give us ten special laws he wanted us to obey. If we obeyed these laws, we would be happy and blessed.

Then God said, "Come up to the top of the mountain, Moses."

So up the mountain I climbed. Up . . . up . . . up into the smoky, misty cloud. For forty wonderful days I stayed on the mountaintop alone with God.

There with his own finger God wrote his ten special laws on two flat pieces of stone. He gave me the pieces of stone to carry back to his people so they would always remember his laws and obey them.

What a wonderful time it was when God talked to me on the mountaintop, high in the clouds, and wrote his ten commandments on the two tablets of stone.

Why did God call Moses up to the top of the mountain? What did God write on the two tablets of stone? Why did God want his people to obey his commandments? If they obeyed them, would they be happy and blessed?

Colored By: _____

Date: _____

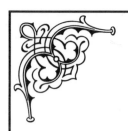
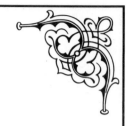

The Fearful Spies and Their Cluster of Grapes
Numbers 13:1 to 14:30

Have you ever seen a grape cluster so big it took two men to carry it? That's what we saw one day in a strange land.

Moses had sent us to spy out the land that God had promised to give us. He said, "See if the people are weak or strong. See if they live in cities or tents. See what grows in their land. Bring back some of their fruit to show us."

For forty days we walked through the land. Before we returned, we picked a cluster of grapes to take back with us. The cluster was so large that one man alone couldn't carry it. We hung the grapes over a pole, and two men walked along, each holding one end of the pole.

When our people saw us returning with the huge cluster of grapes, they were delighted. When we told them that it was a good land with green meadows and sparkling streams, they were pleased. But when we told them that we saw huge giants there—giants so big we felt like grasshoppers beside them—the people cried out, "Let's not enter that land! Those giants would kill us!"

We spies were frightened, too—all except Joshua and Caleb. They trusted God completely. "Don't be afraid!" they told the people. "God has told us to enter the land! Let's go in! God will be with us!"

Sad to say, the rest of us didn't trust God. Because of this, none of the people who refused to obey God were allowed to enter the promised land. Instead God let his people wander in the harsh wilderness for forty more years. How much better it would have been to trust God and spend those forty years enjoying the wonderful, good land God wanted to give us!

What did the spies show their people that made them glad? What did the spies tell their people that made them fearful? Did they trust God to take care of them? Were they ever able to enter the promised land?

Colored By: _____

Date: _____

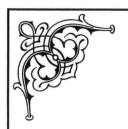
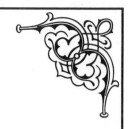

Samson, the Strongest Man Who Ever Lived
Judges 13:1 to 16:31

I was the strongest man who ever lived.

One day when a lion leaped on me, I grabbed it by the jaws and tore it apart! Another time when my enemies tied me in strong ropes, I snapped them apart as easily as if they were threads. Later, when they imprisoned me behind heavy iron gates, I pulled up the gates and carried them away on my shoulders.

What was the secret to my strength?

Before I was born, an angel told my mother that God would use me to save my people from their enemies. The angel said my hair should never be cut. This would show that I had been given to God, and that God was with me in a special way.

One day my enemies discovered the secret to my strength. They crept up when I was sleeping and quietly cut off all my hair. When I awoke, my strength was gone. I was weak. My enemies threw me into prison.

Later they dragged me from prison so they could parade me before a crowd of people feasting in their temple.

But by this time my hair had grown long again, so I prayed, "God, give me strength once more!"

I placed my arms around the pillars which held up the temple roof and pulled with all my might. I was strong again! The pillars collapsed and the roof came crashing down!

Three thousand of God's enemies were killed that day! Just as the angel told my mother many years before, God used me mightily to save my people from their enemies.

What was the secret to Samson's great strength? What great things could he do because he was so strong? What did he do to the ferocious lion in the picture? How did Samson use his great strength to destroy God's enemies?

Colored By: _____

Date: _____

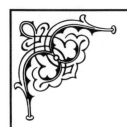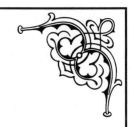

God's Wonderful Answer
to Hannah's Prayer
1 Samuel 1:1-28; 2:18-21

I was a sad wife. More than anything else I wanted a baby. Many times I wept bitterly and would not eat because I had no child.

My husband said, "Hannah, isn't my love enough to make you happy?"

I told him, "I will always feel sad until I have a son."

Every year we journeyed to the house of the Lord to offer sacrifices to our God. As I leaned against the wall of the temple one day, I wept and prayed, "Oh, God! If you will give me a baby boy, I'll give him back to you so he can serve you all the days of his life!"

God heard my prayer. How happy I was when he gave me a baby boy! I named him Samuel.

When Samuel was still a small child, I took him to the temple and presented him to Eli the priest. I said, "This is the son I prayed for as I stood here by the temple one day. God heard my prayer, and now I am giving this child back to the Lord."

From that day on Samuel lived at the temple helping Eli the priest.

Every year my husband and I journeyed to the temple to worship God. Every year I took Samuel a new little coat which I had made for him. The first thing I did when we arrived at the temple was to give Samuel a loving hug. Then I gave him his new little coat.

Though it always made me feel sad to say goodbye to Samuel, I was thankful that God had answered my prayer for a son. I was glad to know that Samuel was happy living at the temple and serving God.

———————

What did Hannah promise to do if God answered her prayer for a baby boy? Did God answer her prayer? Did she keep her promise? What did Hannah give Samuel each time she went to visit him?

Colored By: _____

Date: _____

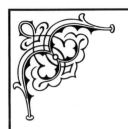
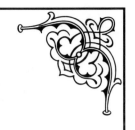

The Shepherd Boy
Who Played for the King
1 Samuel 16:14-23

When Saul became king over Israel, he was wise and humble. Later, however, he grew proud and headstrong. He did not obey God. Because of this, God's Spirit departed from him.

Without God's Spirit upon him, Saul became sad and moody. At other times he was angry and violent.

The king's servants wanted to help their master. "Oh, king," they said, "let us find someone to play on a harp whenever you become sad or angry. Perhaps the music will soothe you."

The king asked, "Can you find such a person?"

A servant replied, "I have heard of a shepherd boy in Bethlehem who plays upon his harp. His name is David, and he is known to be very wise and pleasant."

This pleased the king and he sent for David. So David left his sheep and came to the royal palace of the king.

Whenever Saul became sad, the servants called, "Come quickly, David! Play on your harp!" David hurried to the palace. He sat down before the king and strummed cheerful songs upon his harp. The cheerful music made the king feel cheerful.

Whenever the king became violent and angry, the servants called David. He hurried to the palace. He sat down before the king and strummed peaceful songs upon his harp. The peaceful music made the king feel peaceful.

King Saul grew to love David, not only because his music made him feel cheerful and peaceful, but also because the Lord was with this kind and noble shepherd boy in all that he did.

How did Saul change after he became king? Are proud and headstrong people happy? Was Saul happy? How did David, the shepherd boy, help King Saul when he was sad and angry?

Colored By: _____

Date: _____

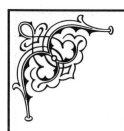
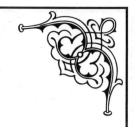

How Young David
Killed Goliath the Giant
1 Samuel 17:1-51

My name is David. I'm just a young shepherd boy, but I'm not afraid to fight the giant Goliath.

Every day Goliath comes out of his camp. He stands at the top of the hill and calls out to the king's army, "Come fight me, you cowards!"

When the soldiers see how big Goliath is, they tremble and run away in fright.

I'm smaller than those soldiers, but I won't run away. I know God will help me just as he always has.

One day a hungry lion and a bear grabbed my little lambs. God helped me fight them off with my bare hands. If God could save me from the lion and the bear, he can save me from this big giant too.

Here comes Goliath now. His sword is sharp and his spear is long. I don't have a sword or a spear. I just have a sling and five smooth stones. But I'm not afraid, for I have God on my side.

Goliath is drawing nearer now! Oh, he's big and tall! He's cursing and sneering at me! His face is fierce and dreadful!

My sling is ready . . . I'm drawing a stone out of my bag . . . I'm closing in on him . . . I'm taking aim . . . and letting go!

ZOOM! The stone is zinging through the air! It's heading straight for Goliath! IT'S HIT THE SPOT!

Hooray! God's enemy has fallen dead!

Thank you, God, for helping me kill the giant!

Thank you, God, for keeping me safe—just as you always have when I put my trust in you!

———————————

What was the only weapon David had when he went to fight the giant? Why was David not afraid of Goliath? Had God helped him before?

Colored By: _____

Date: _____

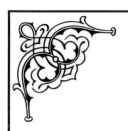
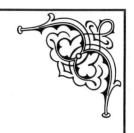

Elijah and the Widow Who Had No Food
1 Kings 17:8-16

A poor widow woman once lived in a land where no grain could grow in the fields because no rain had fallen. She and her small son had barely enough to eat.

One day the poor widow woman went out to gather some sticks to build a fire to cook her last bit of food. On her way she met the prophet Elijah, who was sent to her by God.

"Woman, can you give me some bread?" Elijah asked.

The woman replied, "I have no bread to give you. My cupboards are bare. My flour and oil are almost gone. I'm going home now to build a fire with these two sticks of wood. Then my son and I will eat our last bit of food before we die of hunger."

Elijah said, "Go make your bread and give it to me to eat." The woman was astonished. *This man is asking me to give him our last bite of food?* Then Elijah said, "God has promised me that he will never let your oil run dry or your flour bin become empty!"

The woman believed Elijah's words. She took the last of her flour and oil, baked some bread, and gave it to him. As Elijah was eating it, she ran to look into her flour bin and oil jar. *Would they still be empty?* No, they were full! She cried with joy, for she and her son would not starve after all!

Every day when the widow woman dipped out oil and flour, more oil and flour appeared. Her oil never ran dry, nor did her flour bin ever become empty. Every day when she and her son ate their bread, they bowed their heads and said, "Thank you, God, for our bread! Thank you for sending Elijah to us!"

Why didn't the poor widow woman want to give Elijah any bread? What made her change her mind? Did Elijah's words come true?

Colored By: _____

Date: _____

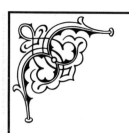
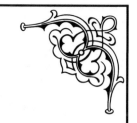

How the Angel Saved Daniel from the Lions
Daniel 6:1-24

My name is Daniel. I am a man who prays to God morning, noon, and night. Nothing can stop me—not even the threat of being eaten by hungry lions.

When the king made me ruler over the land, some jealous men wanted to destroy me. They searched for some misdeed they could report to the king, but could find nothing.

When they noticed that I prayed to God three times a day beside my open window, they said to the king, "Make a law, O king, that anyone who prays to any god or man other than you shall be thrown into the lions' den."

The king foolishly agreed. Then the evil men watched my window, waiting to catch me praying to my God. Did I continue praying as usual? Yes, I did! When they saw me, they grabbed me and carried me off to the king.

"Throw Daniel to the lions!" they cried. "We caught him praying to his God!" The king regretted that he had made the law, but he could not change it. Into the lions' den I was thrown.

All night long the king tossed upon his bed, wondering if the hungry lions were eating me. Early the next morning the king rushed to the den. "Daniel!" he cried. "Has your God saved you from the lions?"

"Yes, O king!" I answered. "My God sent his angel and shut the lions' mouths!"

Rejoicing, the king set me free. Then he ordered the wicked men themselves to be thrown into the lions' den. The hungry lions pounced upon them and ate them all.

Why were the men envious of Daniel? When they couldn't find any misdeed to report to the king, what did they do? Did Daniel stop praying to God? How did God protect Daniel in the lions' den?

Colored By: _____

Date: _____

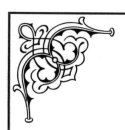
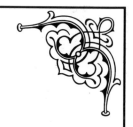

The Fish That Swallowed
Disobedient Jonah
Jonah 1:1 to 2:10

I am a big fish—yes, big enough to swallow a man. And one day that's exactly what I did. I swallowed a man—whole!

As I was swimming in the sea one day, God said, "See that ship up there, tossing in the stormy waves? Swim just beneath it. I have a job for you to do."

As I swam beneath the ship, I heard sailors' voices from the deck above. "We must throw you overboard, Jonah!" they said. "If we don't, we will all die! You disobeyed your God. You wouldn't go to Nineveh, so he has sent this storm! OVER YOU GO!"

KER-SPLASH! Down into the water came Jonah! Down . . . down until he was right in front of me. I knew what God wanted me to do. I opened my jaws wide, took a big gulp, and *swallowed Jonah*! With a swish, he slid into my big empty belly!

For three days and three nights Jonah lay inside my dark, slimy belly. What was he doing? He was praying. When Jonah told God he was sorry he had disobeyed him, God ordered me to swim to the shore and spit out Jonah.

I took a deep breath and spewed Jonah right out of my wide-open mouth! Jonah gushed out onto the sand and scrambled happily to his feet.

As I swam out to sea, I looked back to see what Jonah was doing. He was shaking water from his clothes and heading toward Nineveh to preach to the people there.

I was happy that God could use a big fish like me to teach Jonah that it is always best to obey God.

It was best for Jonah to obey God. Is it always best for children also? Whom else does God tell children to obey? The Bible says, "Children, obey your parents in the Lord."

Colored By: _____

Date: _____

Part 2

NEW
TESTAMENT
BIBLE STORIES

with

Keepsake

Pictures

to
Color

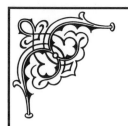
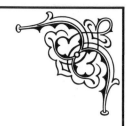

The Angel's Message
to the Shepherds
Luke 2:8-15

It's nighttime. Stars are twinkling above me as I watch over my sheep. Other shepherds are here too, guarding their flocks. It's peaceful here in the fields near Bethlehem. The night is hushed and still—almost as though it is waiting for something special to happen.

What do I see in the sky? It's a bright light shining all around! It's almost blinding me! All the shepherds are jumping to their feet.

Look! An angel has appeared before us! I'm frightened! I'm shaking from head to foot! But listen, the angel is speaking: "Don't be afraid! I am bringing you wonderful news that will fill you with great joy! Tonight in the city of Bethlehem a Savior has been born, who is Christ the Lord! You shall find the baby wrapped in swaddling clothes lying in a manger."

This is truly good news!

Oh, look! The sky is filling with angels! Angels everywhere! Hundreds of them! They're singing "Glory to God in the highest!" Never has there been such a night as this with such wonderful praise ringing out from the skies above us!

The music is fading away now . . . the light is disappearing. The angels have vanished from our sight. Everything is hushed and still again, just like it was before.

"Come on, shepherds! Let's hurry to Bethlehem! It won't be hard to find the Savior. We'll just look for a newborn baby lying in a manger. Who ever heard of a baby sleeping where cattle are fed? Come on! Let's hurry! Let's welcome our newborn King into the world, for he is our Savior and our Lord!"

What were the shepherds doing in the fields that night? What was the good news the angel told the shepherds? In what town was the baby born? Where would the shepherds find him sleeping?

Colored By: _____

Date: _____

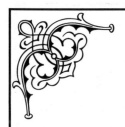
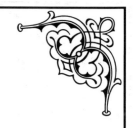

The Wonderful Night
When Jesus Was Born
Luke 2:1-7,15-20

What a wonderful night it was when Jesus was born!

Mary and I had traveled all day to go to Bethlehem to write our names in a book, as the Emperor had ordered. Other people had come to Bethlehem too. The town was crowded. I knocked on the door of the inn. "Do you have a room?" I asked.

"No, nothing at all!" replied the innkeeper. "Every room in Bethlehem is filled tonight!"

Then the innkeeper looked out at Mary. He felt sorry for her. "You can sleep in my stable," he offered. "That's all I have."

So Mary lay down to rest that evening on a bed of straw in a stable where cattle slept.

Later that night the wonderful promise came true. God sent his Son into the world to be born a tiny baby.

After wrapping the babe in swaddling clothes, we looked around for a place to lay him. We used the manger for a crib. It was all we had. I placed clean straw in the manger, and there we laid the baby Jesus.

As Mary and I stood looking down at the baby sleeping on the hay, we heard footsteps approaching. It was shepherds. What were they so excited about? Why had they left their flocks?

The shepherds ran over to look in the manger. When they saw the baby lying there, they cried out with joy. "What the angels told us is true! God has sent his Son into the world to be our Savior!" They knelt before the newborn babe, praising God for his wonderful gift.

Yes, it was a wonderful night when Jesus was born!

Can you memorize this verse? "God so loved the world that he gave his only begotten Son, that whosoever believeth in him should not perish but have everlasting life" (John 3:16).

Colored By: _____

Date: _____

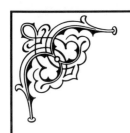
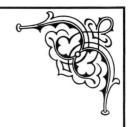

Follow Me and I Will Make You Fishers of Men
Luke 5:1-11

Have you ever gone fishing with your father? Have you ever sat by the river for hours without catching any fish? Then you'll know how Peter and his brother Andrew felt after fishing all night without catching one fish.

Over and over again they pulled up their net, only to find it empty. When morning came, they were discouraged. They wanted to give up and go home.

Jesus was nearby when they returned to shore. He looked at their empty nets. "Take your boat out into the deep and let down your nets to catch some fish," he said.

"But Master," Peter replied, "Andrew and I have fished all night and we haven't caught one fish! But if you say so, we'll try again."

So again they went out in their boat. Again they threw in their net. But this time when they pulled up their net, they were amazed. The net was full of fish! In fact, it was so full that the net began to break!

They called over to James and John, who were fishing nearby. "Come help us!" When James and John came up beside them, they loaded both of their boats so full of fish that the boats began to sink.

Returning to shore, Peter fell down at Jesus' feet. Overwhelmed by his great power, Peter cried out, "Depart from me, Lord. I'm not even worthy to be near you!"

But Jesus had wonderful plans for Peter and his brother Andrew. He wanted them to become his helpers. "Come follow me," he said, "and I will make you fishers of men." Immediately they left their nets and followed him.

Does Jesus want each of us to follow him? How can we become "fishers of men"? Can you tell others that Jesus loves them and wants to be their Savior?

Colored By: _____

Date: _____

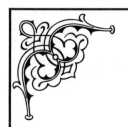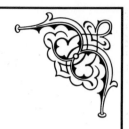

The Man Who Came Down Through the Roof
Luke 5:18-26

I lay upon my sickbed, wishing I could go see Jesus. I knew that Jesus could speak a word and make me well. But I couldn't go to Jesus. My legs wouldn't carry me. I couldn't walk at all.

My four friends felt sorry for me. They said, "We'll carry you in your bed!" So down the street they carried me.

I was excited. "I'm going to see Jesus! Jesus heals the sick and the lame! Jesus will make me walk again!"

When we arrived at the house, we found a huge crowd outside the door. We couldn't get in. I was disappointed. "I can't get to Jesus after all. I'll never walk again. I'll spend my whole life lying on this bed."

"Don't feel bad," my friends said. "If we can't go through the door, we'll go through the roof!"

"Go through the roof? Who ever heard of such a thing?"

But my friends replied, "We'll tear a big hole in the roof and let you down with ropes."

And sure enough, they did! They carefully lowered me down . . . down . . . down . . . into the crowded room until I lay right in front of Jesus. Yes, Jesus was standing right beside me!

Did Jesus heal me? Yes, he did! He said, "Take up your bed and walk!"

I jumped to my feet and I discovered I could walk! My legs were strong again! How happy I was! My four friends were happy too!

I threw my bed mat over my shoulders and started home. But as I walked, I praised the Lord. For now I had two strong legs to take me wherever I chose to go.

How did the sick man travel to the house where Jesus was? How did he get inside the house when he couldn't go through the door? Were the four men who helped him truly good friends? Should friends always help one another?

Colored By: _____

Date: _____

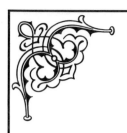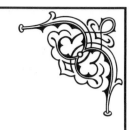

How the Wind and the Waves Obeyed Jesus
Matthew 8:23-27

All day long we had watched Jesus healing the sick, but now it was evening and Jesus was weary. He spoke to us helpers. "Please take me over to the other side of the lake," he said, "so I can get some rest."

As we started rowing across the lake, Jesus lay down on a pillow at the the back of the boat and fell fast asleep.

Suddenly a fierce storm arose. The wind was tossing our boat around! It was tipping and dipping! The waves rose higher and higher until they started rushing right into our boat! Our boat was filling with water! We were sinking!

Terrified, we called to Jesus, who lay asleep in the boat. "Jesus, wake up!" we cried. "We're about to drown! Don't you care about us? Help us! Do something quick! Save us, Lord!"

When Jesus heard our cries, he opened his eyes and looked out over the roaring sea. Then he stood in the boat, pointed to the wind and the waves, and uttered a command. "Quiet down!" he said. "Hush! Be still!"

Suddenly all was calm. The wind stopped its blowing. The waves stopped their dashing. The wind and the waves had instantly obeyed Jesus' command. The lake was smooth and peaceful once again.

Jesus turned to us. "Why did you get so terrified?" he asked. "Why didn't you trust me?"

We looked at one another in amazement and awe, marveling at what we had just seen.

"What kind of man is this?" we said to one another. "He speaks to the wind and the waves, and they obey him!"

Whom did Jesus' helpers turn to when they were afraid? Did Jesus help them in their time of need? When you are afraid, whom can you turn to? Is anything too hard for Jesus to do?

Colored By: _____

Date: _____

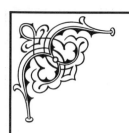
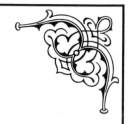

The Little Girl
Who Was Brought Back to Life
Mark 5:22-43

"Jesus!" I cried. "Please come heal my little girl! She's dying!"

Jesus started to follow me home, but people crowded around us. "My daughter will die before Jesus can reach her!" I thought.

A messenger from home pushed through the crowds. "Jairus!" he called. "Your little girl has died. Don't bother Jesus anymore. It's too late. He can't help her now."

My heart was heavy, but Jesus said, "Trust me. Your daughter will be healed."

When we arrived at our house, we heard loud weeping and wailing. "Why are you weeping?" Jesus asked the mourners. "The little girl is going to be well."

The mourners scoffed. "That's ridiculous! Anyone can see that the girl is dead!"

We went with Jesus into our daughter's bedroom. Closing the door, Jesus walked over to the bed where our daughter's lifeless body lay. Taking her by the hand, Jesus commanded, "Little girl, arise!" We held our breath. Would Jesus bring her back from the dead? To our amazement, we saw her eyelids flutter slightly. Then her eyes opened wide. Looking up at Jesus, she gave him a smile, got out of bed, and stood upright on her feet.

"Give her something to eat!" Jesus said. We rushed to bring her food. Our daughter ate! She truly was alive and well!

Tears of joy ran down our cheeks. With grateful hearts we fell on our knees before the Lord. "Thank you, Jesus!" we cried. "Thank you for bringing our daughter back from the dead!"

What did Jesus say to the little girl as she lay dead in her bed? What did the girl do? What did Jesus tell her mother and father to do? Who is it that gives us our life and our breath?

Colored By: _____

Date: _____

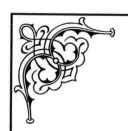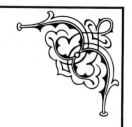

How Jesus Blessed the Little Children
Mark 10:13-16

I am so excited! Mother is taking me to see Jesus. Other mothers are bringing their children, too. Some are carrying tiny babies in their arms. Everyone wants to see Jesus!

There he is! I can see him now! He's sitting by the side of the road beneath that shady tree. Jesus sees us. He's smiling and stretching out his hands toward us. He looks loving and kind!

But oh! What is happening? Jesus' helpers are stepping in front of us! They're pushing us away!

"Go away, children!" they say. "Don't bother the Master! Go away!" They're forcing us back. I'm so disappointed! I feel like crying. I wanted to get close to Jesus.

But Jesus is turning to his helpers now. He looks unhappy. He's scolding them.

"Don't send the children away," he's saying. "Let the little children come to me!" He's beckoning to us!

Jesus does want us after all! I'm drawing closer to him now. He's smiling at me and lifting me up onto his lap. He's laying his hands upon me and asking God to bless me!

"God in heaven," he's praying, "bless this precious child. May your love surround her each day of her life. May she always do the things that please you!" His voice is soft and gentle. I feel his great love for me.

Now he's blessing the other children too—every one of them, big and small! I'm happy now, for I know that Jesus loves all children everywhere! I know he loves me, too!

Do you know the song "Jesus Loves Me"? While you are singing the song, look at the picture of Jesus blessing the children. Can you imagine that you were one of the children?

Colored By: _____

Date: _____

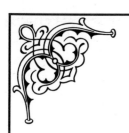
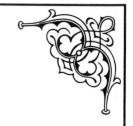

The Boy Who Gave His Lunch to Jesus
John 6:1-14

"Come with us to hear Jesus!" my neighbors called as they passed by my door.

"Mother, may I go?"

"Yes," she replied, "but you must take a lunch with you."

I placed five little loaves of bread and two fish in a basket, and off I went with my neighbors to see Jesus. By the time we arrived at the grassy hill where Jesus was teaching, a huge crowd had gathered. Time passed quickly. Soon everyone was hungry.

"Send the people away so they can get some food!" Jesus' helpers told him.

But Jesus answered, "You can give them food!"

"But how can we do that?" asked his puzzled helpers.

"Sir," I said, "I have a lunch here. But it's just five loaves and two fish." When the helper told Jesus about my lunch, he took my lunch in his hands, blessed it, and started breaking it into pieces to give to the hungry people.

"My lunch won't feed very many people," I thought, "even if they take only tiny bites!" But as I watched, an amazing thing took place before my eyes! No matter how many pieces Jesus broke off from my lunch, there was always more left! More . . . and more . . . and MORE! There was enough to feed everyone all they could eat!

I couldn't wait to arrive home and tell my mother. When she heard that Jesus had fed five thousand people with my lunch, she hugged me tight. She was glad I had given my lunch to Jesus. I was glad, too!

Look at the picture. How many loaves does the boy have in his lunch basket? How many fish? How many people did Jesus feed with this small lunch? This is called "The Miracle of the Loaves and Fishes." What is a miracle?

Colored By: _____

Date: _____

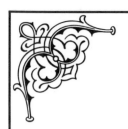
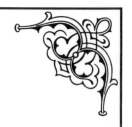

How Peter Walked
on the Water to Jesus
Matthew 14:22-33

Where do people usually walk? People walk on the ground. People walk on floors, sidewalks, and streets. But do people walk on water? Never! At least, that's what I thought until one night when I was in a boat with Jesus' helpers out on a stormy lake.

We had been struggling for hours trying to row our boat against the wind and the waves. About midnight we saw a figure walking toward us on the water—on top of the swirling waves! Was it a ghost? We screamed aloud in terror!

Then we heard Jesus' voice. "Don't be afraid," he called out. "It is I!"

I answered him, "Lord, if it is really you, tell me to walk out to you upon the water!"

"Come, Peter!" Jesus replied. I jumped out of the boat onto the angry sea. Did my feet sink in the water? No! It was just like walking on solid ground! With my eyes fixed on Jesus, I walked toward him on top of the water.

Then I looked down at the wild waves slapping around my feet. I became frightened! I started sinking down, down, down into the deep sea!

"Save me, Lord!" I cried out in terror. Instantly Jesus reached out his hand and lifted me up out of the waves.

"Why did you start to doubt, Peter?" he asked me.

When Jesus and I boarded the boat, the sea became calm. The storm ceased. Jesus' helpers and I were astonished to see Jesus' power. We fell down before him saying, "Truly you are the Son of God!"

Where was Peter looking when he walked on the water? Where was Peter looking when he began to sink down into the angry waves? When we are afraid, is it best to think about the things we fear, or about Jesus?

Colored By: _____

Date: _____

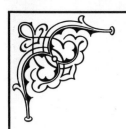
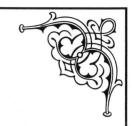

Jesus' Visit in the Home
of Mary and Martha
Luke 10:38-42

Jesus is coming to have dinner with us! My sister, Mary, and I love to have Jesus visit us here in our home. But sometimes I worry about what to serve him for dinner.

Mary always says, "Don't worry, Martha! The most important thing isn't what we eat. The most important thing is that Jesus is with us and we can listen to his wonderful words."

Of course, Jesus' words are wonderful. No man ever spoke like he does. Yet I do want to serve Jesus a nice dinner so that he'll enjoy it.

Oh, here comes Jesus now. Mary is opening the door for him. I mustn't leave the kitchen, or my food might burn. I see that Mary has sat down beside Jesus. She's listening to him. It would be nice to hear what he's telling her, but someone has to stay in the kitchen.

Oh, dear! The meat is burning! How can I watch the meat and peel the vegetables too? And the table needs setting! Why doesn't my sister help me? Here I am scurrying around and she's resting comfortably, smiling up at Jesus. It isn't fair! I'm going to speak to Jesus about it.

"Jesus, don't you care that my sister has left me to do all this work alone? Tell Mary to come help me!"

Jesus is looking at me sadly. "Martha, Martha!" he says. "You are worried and upset about many things, but only one thing is important. And Mary has chosen the most important thing—to listen to my words. For my words will always remain in her heart. They will never be taken away from her."

––––––––––––

There are many good things we enjoy doing. But what is the most important thing we can ever do? Do you like to listen to Jesus' words? How do we hear them?

Colored By: _____

Date: _____

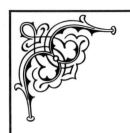
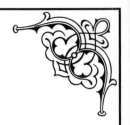

The Good Samaritan
Who Helped a Wounded Man
Luke 10:30-37

I must hurry! The sun is going down! It's dangerous to be traveling alone on this road at night, for robbers hide behind the rocks.

What's that noise? Oh, it's the robbers!

Help! They're leaping out at me! They're waving clubs in the air! They're grabbing me and beating me! They're stripping off my clothes and running away with all my money!

Now they've left me here beside the road! I'm groaning in pain! Will I die here all alone?

I hear footsteps! Someone is coming down the road. *"Help me! I'm dying!"* The traveler doesn't even want to look at me. He's crossing to the other side.

I hear more footsteps! Maybe this one will take pity on me. *"Help me! Please!"* No, he's passing by me too.

I hear footsteps again, but I suppose this man will go on his way just like the others. The footsteps are coming closer now. They're stopping! The man wants to help me!

I see a kind face above me, and I hear a gentle voice. The man is pouring oil on my wounds and placing me on his donkey. How kind he is. He's taking me to an inn for the night so I'll have a bed to sleep in. In the morning the kind man will go on his way, but he's told the innkeeper to let me stay here until I feel better, and he will pay any extra charges when he returns.

I ask you a question: Which of these three men was a good neighbor to me? The one who was merciful and kind, of course—the good Samaritan.

How can you be kind to people needing help? If your mother is sick in bed, how could you help her? If a neighbor lady stumbles and drops her packages, what could you do?

Colored By: _____

Date: _____

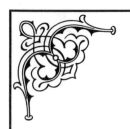
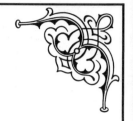

The Dead Man Who
Walked Out of His Grave
John 11:1-45

Mary was sitting in her house weeping. Her brother Lazarus had died and friends were trying to comfort her. "If Jesus had only been here," Mary sobbed, "he could have healed my brother. But now Lazarus is dead and buried."

Mary's sister, Martha, rushed into the house. "Mary," she cried, "Jesus has arrived! He's asking for you! Dry your tears and come with me!" Mary arose and went with her sister. Their friends followed them. When Mary saw Jesus, she fell at his feet.

"Lord," she sobbed brokenheartedly, "if you had only been here, my brother would not have died!"

Jesus felt sad to see Mary's tears. "Where is he buried?" he asked. They led him to the cave. "Take away the stone," he ordered. The men rolled it away. Jesus lifted up his eyes toward heaven. "Father, I thank you that you always hear me when I pray." Then with a loud voice he commanded, "LAZARUS, COME FORTH!"

The people were dumbfounded. *Was Jesus really expecting a man who had been dead for four days to walk out of his grave?* They stared intently at the cave.

Then it happened! They saw it with their own eyes! There at the door of the cave a man appeared, wrapped head to feet in graveclothes!

"Look! Look!" the people shouted. "It's Lazarus! He's alive!" Yes, Lazarus had indeed come forth from the grave!

Mary and Martha were filled with joy. "Our brother is alive!" they cried. "Thank you, Jesus!"

The people watching said, "Truly Jesus is the Son of God! Who else could raise the dead?"

Is there anything at all that is too hard for Jesus to do?

Colored By: _____

Date: _____

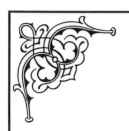
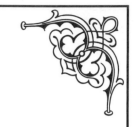

The Little Lost Lamb
and the Good Shepherd
Luke 15:3-7

I'm glad my shepherd led our flock to this green meadow today. We've nibbled grass here all day long. But now the sun is setting. Our shepherd will soon be leading us back to the fold, where we'll be safe for the night. Our shepherd has a large flock of sheep to take care of—one hundred of us! But our shepherd knows each one of us by name.

All the other sheep are resting right now, but I don't feel tired at all. I wonder what lies beyond that hill over there. I think I'll go see for myself!

Hmmm . . . it's much farther than I thought!

OUCH! These thorns are stabbing me! Oh, dear! Now I'm caught in these prickly bushes! I'm tugging and struggling but I can't get loose! What is going to happen to me out here all alone? It's getting dark. What do I hear? It's wolves howling! I'm frightened! Wolves like to eat little lambs like me.

Has my shepherd noticed that I'm missing? The other ninety-nine sheep are all safe in the fold by now, but here I am hurt and bleeding.

What do I hear? It's footsteps! Could my shepherd be looking for me? Yes! It's my shepherd! I hear his voice! He's calling "Little lamb! Little lamb!" I'll try to answer him. "BAAA . . . BAAA!"

Does he hear me? Yes! He's running toward me! *He's found me!* Oh, how good it feels to be lifted up into my shepherd's strong and loving arms! I feel safe and happy now. What a wonderful shepherd I have. He cares about each sheep in his flock. Even though he has ninety-nine other sheep, he still cares for a little lost lamb like me.

The Bible tells us that Jesus is our "Good Shepherd." What does that tell us about Jesus? Does Jesus care for each one of us? Does he care for his little ones? Does he care for you?

Colored By: _____

Date: _____

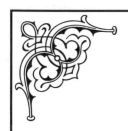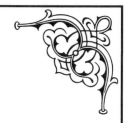

The Sad Son
Who Left His Father's House
Luke 15:11-24

Here I sit in a pigpen, feeding these hungry pigs.

They're grunting happily as they gobble up these corn husks, but I'm not happy. I'm so hungry I could eat this pig food myself!

I wish I were back in my father's house! Why did I ever leave home?

I asked my father to give me my share of the money, and he did. But the money's all gone now. I wasted it on wild and wicked things.

Now I'm here in this pigpen, sad and hungry, remembering all the good food in my father's house. Even his servants had plenty to eat.

I know what I'll do! I'll return home! I'll ask my father to hire me as one of his servants. I've done so many wrong things, I'm no longer worthy to be his son.

The way is long and weary, but I'm almost home. What do I see down the road? It's my father!

He's running to meet me! He's welcoming me back home! He's kissing me, and placing a robe on me . . . and shoes on my feet . . . and a ring on my hand!

My father still loves me! He's been watching and waiting for me ever since I went away.

I've told him that I have sinned and am no longer worthy to be called his son, but he has forgiven me! He's planning a great feast for me tonight.

"Everyone come!" he shouts. "My son was gone, but now he's back home again! Come and rejoice with me!"

What a wonderful father I have!

Did the father ever stop loving his son—even when he was doing wicked things? Did the father forgive his son when he returned home? Does God always love us and forgive us when we are sorry for our sins?

Colored By: _____

Date: _____

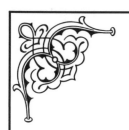
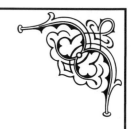

The Blind Man
Whose Eyes Were Opened
Luke 18:35-43

Close your eyes tightly. What can you see? Nothing at all! Nothing but blackness! Before I met Jesus, that was all I ever saw. Just blackness! "Blind Bartimaeus" they called me. Every day I sat beside the road in rags begging for help.

If people walked by, I could hear their voices, but I couldn't see them. If a child reached out to me, I could feel his hand, but I couldn't see him. I couldn't see the sky, the grass, the birds, or the flowers. All I could see was blackness, for I was blind.

One day I heard a crowd gathering nearby. "What's happening?" I asked.

"Jesus is here!" someone answered.

I was excited, for I knew Jesus could heal me. I yelled out, "Jesus, take pity on me! Jesus, help me!"

Someone growled, "Stop it, Bartimaeus! You're yelling too loud!" But I kept on shouting.

Then I heard someone calling for me. "Bartimaeus! Come quickly! Jesus wants to see you!" I sprang to my feet and ran to Jesus.

"What do you want me to do for you?" Jesus asked.

"Oh, Jesus," I begged, "I want to be able to see!"

Jesus reached forth his hands and touched my eyes. "Go on your way now," he said softly. "Your faith has healed you!"

It was true! I was healed! Instantly I could see the sky and the birds! I could see the trees and the flowers! And I could see the happy faces all around me. Everyone was joyfully praising God, and I was too, for Jesus had healed me! Now I could see!

Have you ever thanked God for your eyes? Let's thank him right now. "Thank you, God, for giving me eyes to see the sky, the trees, the birds, and the flowers!"

Colored By: _____

Date: _____

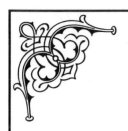
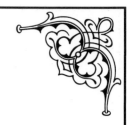

The Man Who
Climbed a Tree to See Jesus
Luke 19:1-10

Oh, how I wish I were taller! I'm standing here by the side of the road waiting to see Jesus. A crowd of other people is waiting here too. They're all in front of me! I'm so short that I won't be able to see over their heads.

Everyone has come here to see Jesus! He heals the sick, makes the blind see, and makes the crippled walk. He even raises the dead!

Jesus is coming closer now! But even if I stand on my toes, I still won't be able to see him. I know what I'll do! I'll climb up into this sycamore tree!

Here I am! I made it just in time. Jesus is almost here. He's coming closer. Now he's right beneath my tree. He's stopping! He's looking up at me! His eyes are full of love. They seem to look clear through me. Jesus is calling me by name! *How did he know my name?* He says, "Come down, Zacchaeus! I'm going to stay at your house today!"

Jesus is coming to *my* house? How wonderful! I must hurry home to prepare a special feast for him! I want everything to be just right for Jesus. But something else needs to be made right. When Jesus looked into my eyes so lovingly, a strange feeling came over me. I remembered all the wrong things I had ever done and I felt sorry about them.

I know what I'll do! I'll return the money I've stolen. And I'll pay back even more than I stole! And I'll give half of my wealth to the poor people. Meeting Jesus has changed my life. I'll never be the same again!

What if Jesus came to your house today? Would you feel bad if you had been doing wrong things? Jesus is always with us. He knows everything we do, say, or think! He always loves us, and he always forgives us when we are sorry.

Colored By: _____

Date: _____

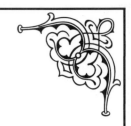

The Young Donkey
Who Carried the Lord Jesus
Luke 19:28-38

Day after day I watched other donkeys carrying people down the road, but no one ever rode on me. I wondered, "Will I soon be big enough so someone can ride on me?"

Then one morning two strangers came. They started untying me. My master said, "What are you doing with my young donkey? Why are you untying him?"

"The Lord has need of him!" the men answered.

"Take him then," my master replied. The men took me away, leading me down the road to where Jesus and his followers were waiting.

Some of Jesus' helpers took off their coats and laid them over my back. I was excited, for I knew they were making a soft cushion for someone to sit on.

In a moment I discovered who that someone was! It was the Lord Jesus himself!

How happy I was to carry Jesus along the road! All the people were happy too. They cut down palm branches from the trees. Some stood waving the palm branches back and forth as we passed by. Others threw them on the road in front of Jesus, singing and cheering.

"Blessed be Jesus, our King!" they shouted. "Hosanna! Glory to God in the highest!"

When we entered the city of Jerusalem, it was like a big parade. Everyone stood beside the road, looking at us and marveling! They said, "Who is this man riding on the donkey?"

"It is the one who performs great wonders and miracles," others answered. "It is Jesus, the Lord!"

If Jesus were to come to your town, would you be happy? How would you greet him? Would you sing and cheer? Why do we call this special day "Palm Sunday"?

Colored By: _____

Date: _____

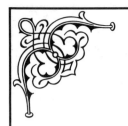
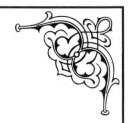

The Angel's Message:
"He Is Not Here! He Is Risen!"
Luke 23:33 to 24:9

"Crucify him! Let him die!" shouted the angry mob.

Cruel soldiers seized the Lord Jesus. They beat him with heavy sticks and placed a crown of thorns on his head. They led him to Calvary, where they nailed him to a wooden cross.

Jesus' mother and other friends watched with heavy hearts as Jesus, who had never done anything wrong, hung on the cross, bled, and died.

Jesus' friends lovingly carried his body to a nearby garden. Here they placed Jesus' body in a cave dug out of rocks. After rolling a heavy stone across the entrance to the cave, they walked sadly back to their homes.

Early Sunday morning, just as the sun was rising, some women came to the garden to care for Jesus' body. They wondered how they could enter the cave. "Who will roll away the stone?" they asked.

When they reached the cave, they were surprised to find the stone already rolled away. They stooped to look inside. "The tomb is empty!" they cried. "Jesus' body is gone!"

Just then their eyes beheld a shining angel. In a triumphant voice the angel announced, "Jesus is not here . . . he is risen!"

Filled with joy, the women ran to tell others the good news. "Jesus is *alive!*" they cried. "He's *alive!* God has raised him from the dead!"

Jesus' friends rejoiced. Their sad hearts were now full of wonder and praise. For this was the most wonderful news they had ever heard! Jesus was alive! He had risen from the grave!

―――――――――

What do we celebrate on Easter? Why is Easter the most joyous holiday of our year? Where is Jesus today? Does he hear us when we pray to him? Will he return to earth again someday?

Colored By: _____

Date: _____

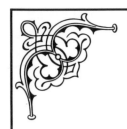
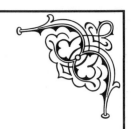

How the Angel
Rescued Peter from Prison
Acts 12:1-11

Everyone is asleep, but I'm lying here on a hard prison floor thinking about the exciting things that happened today.

I was on the streets preaching about Jesus when suddenly soldiers broke through the crowd of people who were listening to me. The soldiers grabbed me and threw me into this prison. "No more preaching!" they warned. "King Herod doesn't want you preaching about Jesus!" Do they think their threats will stop me? No, I'll never stop telling people about the Savior. No, never!

This cold, hard floor isn't a comfortable bed, but I'm so tired, I can't stay awake. I'll pray, then I'll try to go to sleep.

"God, I thank you that I could tell others about Jesus today. I know you will take care of me through this night. Amen."

Something is waking me! It's a blazing light! It's an angel! He's saying, "Get up and get dressed!" *Get dressed? With my hands and feet in these heavy chains?* The angel is stretching out his hand toward me, and the chains are breaking apart!

The angel says, "Quick! Follow me!" I'm scrambling into my clothes. It feels good to be able to stretch my legs again.

We're hurrying through the prison yard now. We're almost at the gate! The gate is made of heavy iron, and it's locked. But the angel is touching it. The lock is snapping and the iron gate is swinging wide open! I'm free! I'm walking out into the dark city streets—a free man! Praise God! He sent his angel to deliver me from prison!

Now I can tell others about Jesus. Everyone needs to hear about Jesus, for he is God's Son and the Savior of the world!

Why was Peter thrown in jail? Will that stop him from telling people about Jesus? How did Peter's chains break apart? How did the iron gate open? Who sent the angel to deliver Peter? Wasn't God good to take care of Peter?

96

Colored By: _____

Date: _____

Part 3

MY
Very Own

Keepsake Drawings

of the
Wonderful World
God
Created

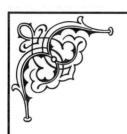
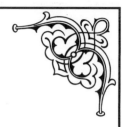

I Can Draw a Picture of the Earth and the Sea

In the beginning God created the heaven and the earth.
—Genesis 1:1

And God said, "Let the waters under the heaven
be gathered together unto one place,
and let the dry land appear";
and it was so.
And God called the dry land Earth,
and the gathering together of the waters called he Seas.
And God saw that it was good.
—Genesis 1:9,10

• Can you draw a picture of the earth?
  Can you show the hills and valleys and mountains that cover the earth?

• Can you draw the sea?
  Can you show the wide ocean with its rolling waves?

My Very Own
Keepsake Drawings

This is a Picture of: _____

_____

Drawn By: _____ Date: _____

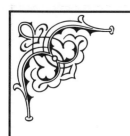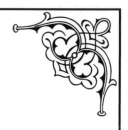

I Can Draw a Picture of Things That Grow

And God said, "Let the earth bring forth grass,
the herb yielding seed,
and the fruit tree yielding fruit after his kind,
whose seed is in itself, upon the earth"; and it was so.
—Genesis 1:11

And out of the ground made the LORD God to grow
every tree that is pleasant to the sight,
and good for food.
—Genesis 2:9

- Can you draw a picture of something God made to grow on this earth? Trees or flowers? Daffodils or daisies or tulips? Fields of grass and grain?

- Can you draw some fruit or vegetables God gave us? The corn or the pumpkins you enjoy in the fall? Or the watermelons and berries you eat in the summer?

My Very Own

Keepsake Drawings

This is a Picture of: _____

_____

Drawn By: _____ Date: _____

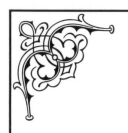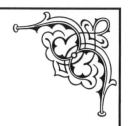

I Can Draw a Picture of the Sun, Moon, and Stars

And God made two great lights;
the greater light to rule the day,
and the lesser light to rule the night;
he made the stars also.
—Genesis 1:16

And God set them
in the firmament of the heaven
to give light upon the earth,
and to rule over the day and over the night,
and to divide the light from the darkness;
and God saw that it was good.
—Genesis 1:17,18

• What was the lesser light that shines at night?
Can you draw a nighttime picture of a child looking at the moon and the stars?

• What was the greater light that shines in the day?
Can you draw a picture of children playing outside with the sun shining overhead?

My Very Own
Keepsake Drawings

This is a Picture of: _____

_____

Drawn By: _____ Date: _____

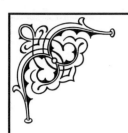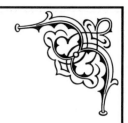

I Can Draw a Picture of Things That Swim or Fly

*And God said,
"Let the waters bring forth abundantly
the moving creature that hath life,
and fowl that may fly above the earth
in the open firmament of heaven."
—Genesis 1:20*

*And God created great whales,
and every living creature that moveth,
which the waters brought forth abundantly,
after their kind,
and every winged fowl after his kind;
and God saw that it was good.
—Genesis 1:21*

- God created many different creatures that live in the water. Can you draw a fish or a frog? A whale or an octopus? A crocodile or a turtle?

- God also created many birds with feathers that fly above the earth. Can you draw a robin or a swallow? A dove or an owl? A duck or a goose?

My Very Own

Keepsake Drawings

This is a Picture of: _____

_____

Drawn By: _____ Date: _____

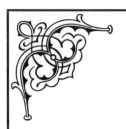
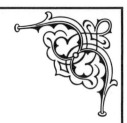

I Can Draw a Picture
of Animals
Wild or Tame

And God said,
"Let the earth bring forth the living creature
after his kind, cattle, and creeping thing,
and beast of the earth
after his kind"; and it was so.
—Genesis 1:24

And God made
the beast of the earth after his kind,
and cattle after their kind, and every thing
that creepeth upon the earth after his kind;
and God saw that it was good.
—Genesis 1:25

- God created every wild animal that lives in the jungles or forests—bears, monkeys, lions, tigers, and elephants. Can you draw a favorite wild animal?

- God created tame animals—cows to give us milk, sheep to give us wool, horses and donkeys to carry our loads. Can you draw a favorite tame animal?

My Very Own

Keepsake Drawings

This is a Picture of: _____

_____

Drawn By: _____ Date: _____

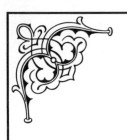
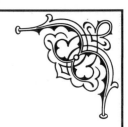

I Can Draw a Picture of Someone God Made: ME!

---

*And God said, "Let us make man in our image,
after our likeness; and let them have dominion
over the fish of the sea, and over the fowl of the air,
and over the cattle, and over all the earth,
and over every creeping thing
that creepeth upon the earth."*
—Genesis 1:26

*So God created man in his
own image, in the image of God created he him;
male and female created he them.*
—Genesis 1:27

• After God made the earth and the seas, the trees and flowers, the fruit and vegetables, the sun and the moon, the fish and the birds, and all the animals . . . then God made man to be his highest creation. Unlike the other creatures and animals, man was given a mind and soul and spirit that could love and worship God.

• When the Bible says God made "man," that includes every boy and girl. That means God made YOU! Can you draw a picture of yourself?

My Very Own

Keepsake Drawings

This is a Picture of: _____

_____

Drawn By: _____ Date: _____